HOW TO MAKE NATURAL FACE CLEANSERS

DR MIRIAM KINAI

ISBN: 1493587633

ISBN-13: 978-1493587636

CONTENTS

1

EQUIPMENT

Liquid Castile Soap Equipment

Apron, safety goggles, heavy duty rubber gloves

Kitchen scale

Stainless steel pot

Large plastic bowl

Plastic pitcher

Stick blender or long handled plastic stirring spoon

Glass covered kitchen thermometer

Soap mold or plastic container

Plastic bag for lining your soap mold

Sharp knife

Natural Face Wash Equipment

Pump bottle

2

INGREDIENTS

Castile Soap Ingredients

16 oz. (454 grams) olive oil

2.0 oz. (58 grams) lye or Sodium hydroxide (NaOH)

6 oz. (159 grams) water

Natural Face Wash Ingredients

2 oz. (60 ml) tablespoons healing fluid like glycerine or green tea

2 oz. (60 ml) tablespoons vegetable oils like jojoba

50 drops of essential oils like lavender and rosemary

1 teaspoon vitamin E oil (optional natural preservative)

* * * * *

3

INSTRUCTIONS

Liquid Castile Soap Instructions

1. Put on your heavy duty plastic gloves and safety goggles.

2. Line your soap mold with the plastic bag so that your soap will unmold easily.

3. Measure out your ingredients

4. Put your olive oil in the stainless steel pot and warm it to 120 degrees Fahrenheit (49 degrees Celsius). Remove them from the heat and let it cool to 110 degrees Fahrenheit (43 degrees Celsius).

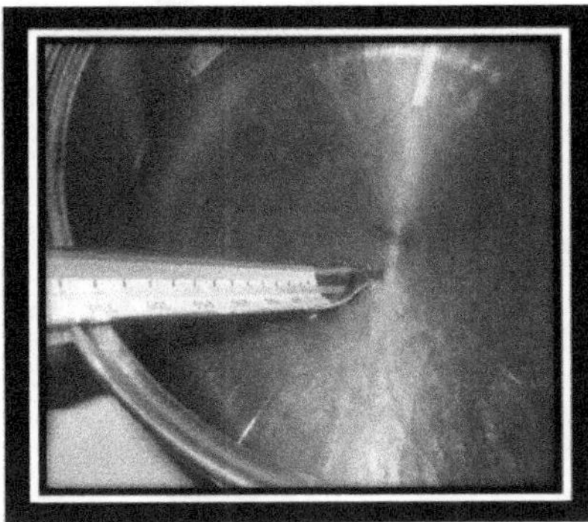

5. Pour your water into the large plastic bowl

6. Add the lye to the water

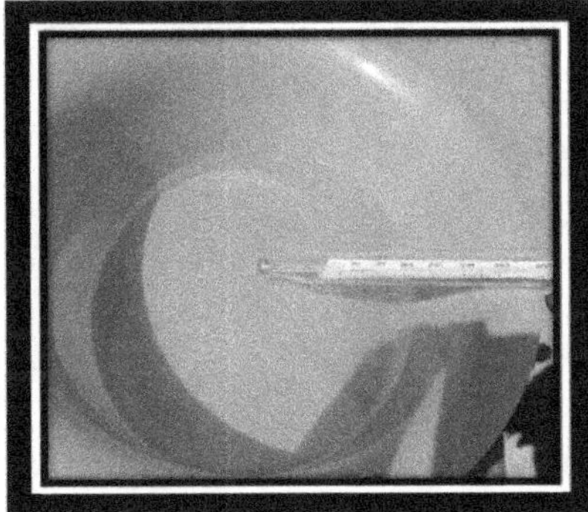

7. Stir it with the stick blender or the long handled plastic spoon and leave the mixture in a well ventilated place so that it can cool to 110 degrees Fahrenheit (43 degrees Celsius).

8. Pour the lye mixture at 110 degrees Fahrenheit (43 degrees Celsius) into the heated oil which should also be at 110 degrees Fahrenheit (43 degrees Celsius) slowly while stirring.

9. Blend or stir the mixture until it traces or develops the consistency of a thick pudding.

10. Once it traces, pour the soap into your soap molds or a plastic container and cover it with a plastic wrap or bag.

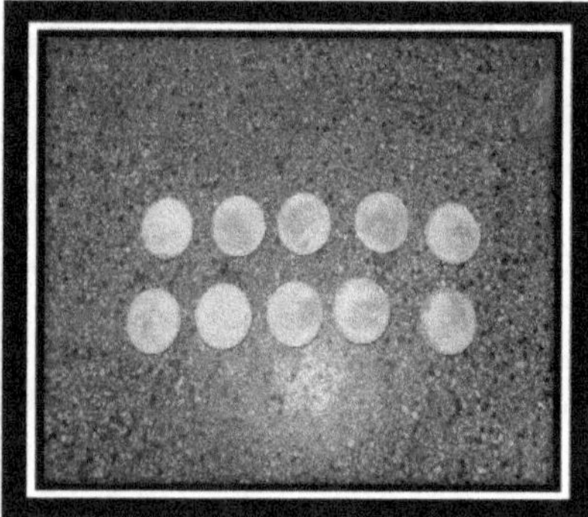

11. Let it cure for 3 days in a well ventilated place before you remove the soap from the mold.

12. Let the large block of soap dry for 24 hours before you cut it into bars.

13. After cutting it into bars, let it cure for 30 days in a well ventilated place before you can use it. Turn the soaps over regularly to ensure each side is well exposed to air.

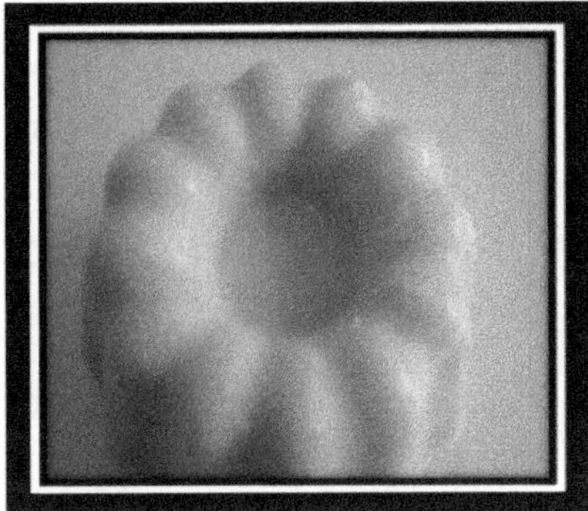

14. After it has cured, use the pure natural soap to make liquid castile soap by grating the bars of soap or cutting them into small pieces.

15. Boil some water and add it to the soap at a ratio of 1 part soap to 3 parts boiling water.

16. Stir the mixture to help it dissolve or just leave it covered in a cool place overnight to dissolve and give you pure Castile liquid soap.

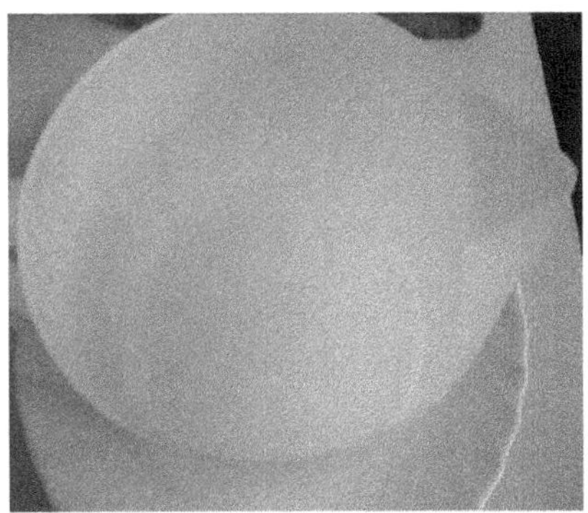

Natural Face Wash Instructions

17. To make natural face cleanser mix the following in a pump bottle:

8 oz. (240 ml or 1 cup) liquid castile soap

2 oz. (60 ml or ¼ cup) healing fluid like glycerine or strong green tea

2 oz. (60 ml or ¼ cup) vegetable oils like sweet almond oil and jojoba

50 drops of essential oils like lavender and rosemary

1 teaspoon vitamin E oil (optional natural preservative)

Tips

You can make a large batch by mixing the liquid Castile soap + vegetable oils + essential oils + vitamin E oil (if using) in a pump bottle.

Store your healing fluids in a separate bottle especially if you are using perishable ones like green tea.

When you need to clean your face mix one part (1 teaspoon) of the healing fluids with 10 parts (10 teaspoons) of the Castile soap + vegetable oils + essential oils mixture.

4

THERAPEUTIC FACE CLEANSER RECIPES

Normal Skin Recipe

8 oz. (240 ml or 1 cup) liquid castile soap

2 oz. (60 ml or ¼ cup) healing fluid that is perfect for normal skin like glycerine, green tea, water, aloe vera gel, rose water, honey

2 oz. (60 ml or ¼ cup) vegetable oils that can be used on normal skin like jojobo, sweet almond oil, virgin coconut, olive oil, sunflower oil, apricot kernel oil, sweet almond, avocado oil

50 drops of essential oils that can be used on normal skin like clary sage, eucalyptus, geranium, grapefruit, lavender, lemon, lemongrass, Roman chamomile, spearmint, sweet orange, rosemary, peppermint, tea tree and ylang ylang

1 teaspoon vitamin E oil (optional natural preservative)

Follow the above Basic Face Wash Recipe Instructions.

***

Oily and Acne Prone Skin Recipe

8 oz. (240 ml or 1 cup) liquid castile soap

2 oz. (60 ml or ¼ cup) healing agent that is perfect for oily skin like aloe vera gel, honey, yogurt, milk (whole and skim), buttermilk, apple juice, lemon juice, neem tea

2 oz. (60 ml or ¼ cup) vegetable oils vegetable oils that are perfect for oily skin like jojoba, sweet almond oil

50 drops of essential oils used to manage oily skin and acne like tea tree, lemon, lavender, sandalwood

1 teaspoon vitamin E oil (optional natural preservative)

Follow the above Basic Face Wash Recipe Instructions.

***

Dry Skin Recipe

8 oz. (240 ml or 1 cup) liquid castile soap

2 oz. (60 ml or ¼ cup) healing fluid that is perfect for dry skin like water, aloe vera gel, glycerine, rose water, honey, yogurt, milk (whole and skim), buttermilk

2 oz. (60 ml or ¼ cup) vegetable oils that are perfect for dry skin like sweet almond oil, sunflower oil, jojoba, avocado oil, apricot kernel, olive, evening primrose, virgin coconut, fractionated coconut oil, calendula oil

50 drops of essential oils used to manage dry skin like lavender, Roman chamomile, ylang ylang

1 teaspoon vitamin E oil (optional natural preservative)

Follow the above Basic Face Wash Recipe Instructions.

***

Sensitive Skin Recipe

8 oz. (240 ml or 1 cup) liquid castile soap

2 oz. (60 ml or ¼ cup) healing fluid that is perfect for sensitive skin like water, aloe vera gel, glycerine, rose water, honey

2 oz. (60 ml or ¼ cup) vegetable oils that are perfect for sensitive skin like apricot kernel oil, sweet almond, avocado oil

50 drops of essential oils used to manage sensitive skin like lavender, Roman chamomile

1 teaspoon vitamin E oil (optional natural preservative)

Follow the above Basic Face Wash Recipe Instructions.

***

Mature Skin Recipe

8 oz. (240 ml or 1 cup) liquid castile soap

2 oz. (60 ml or ¼ cup) healing fluid that is perfect for mature skin like strong green tea, water, aloe vera gel, glycerine, rose water, honey, yogurt, milk (whole and skim), buttermilk, apple juice

2 oz. (60 ml or ¼ cup) vegetable oils that are perfect for mature skin like evening primrose, avocado, apricot kernel, jojoba, sweet almond, olive

50 drops of essential oils used to manage mature skin like rose, geranium, clary sage, lavender essential oils

1 teaspoon vitamin E oil (optional natural preservative)

Follow the above Basic Face Wash Recipe Instructions.

***

Prematurely Aging Skin Recipe

8 oz. (240 ml or 1 cup) liquid castile soap

2 oz. (60 ml or ¼ cup) healing fluid that is perfect for prematurely aging skin strong green tea, water, aloe vera gel, glycerine, rose water, honey, yogurt, milk (whole and skim), buttermilk, apple juice

2 oz. (60 ml or ¼ cup) vegetable oils that are perfect for prematurely aging skin like apricot kernel, carrot, wheat germ, evening primrose, sweet almond oil

50 drops of essential oils used to manage prematurely aging skin like patchouli, clary sage, rose, lavender, geranium

1 teaspoon vitamin E oil (optional natural preservative)

Follow the above Basic Face Wash Recipe Instructions.

***

Eczema Prone Skin Recipe

8 oz. (240 ml or 1 cup) liquid castile soap

2 oz. (60 ml or ¼ cup) healing fluid that is perfect for eczema prone skin like water, aloe vera gel, honey, yogurt, milk (whole and skim)

2 oz. (60 ml or ¼ cup) vegetable oils used to manage eczema like evening primrose oil, rose hip oil, cranberry seed oil, calendula, coconut oil, sweet almond oil, borage seed oil and jojoba

50 drops of essential oils used to manage eczema like geranium, lavender, Roman chamomile and rosemary

1 teaspoon vitamin E oil (optional natural preservative)

Follow the above Basic Face Wash Recipe Instructions.

***

Psoriasis Prone Skin Recipe

8 oz. (240 ml or 1 cup) liquid castile soap

2 oz. (60 ml or ¼ cup) healing fluid that is perfect for psoriasis prone skin like water, aloe vera gel, honey, yogurt, milk (whole and skim)

2 oz. (60 ml or ¼ cup) vegetable oils used to manage psoriasis like cranberry seed oil, borage seed oil, evening primrose oil, calendula, carrot seed oil, jojoba and coconut oil

50 drops of essential oils used to manage psoriasis like bergamot, tea tree, lavender, German chamomile, helichrysum, patchouli, rose and sandalwood

1 teaspoon vitamin E oil (optional natural preservative)

Follow the above Basic Face Wash Recipe Instructions.

***

Coffee Lovers Recipe

8 oz. (240 ml or 1 cup) liquid castile soap

2 oz. (60 ml or ¼ cup) strong coffee

2 oz. (60 ml or ¼ cup) coffee infused vegetable oils. To make your own add ½ cup ground coffee to 1 cup of a vegetable oil like sweet almond oil, olive or sunflower oil. Leave the mixture in a bright sunny place for two to six weeks as you shake it daily – the longer you leave it the stronger it gets. Strain the mixture with a cheese cloth and use the oil in your recipe.

1 teaspoon vitamin E oil (optional natural preservative)

Follow the above Basic Face Wash Recipe Instructions.

***

Chocoholics Recipe

8 oz. (240 ml or 1 cup) liquid castile soap

2 oz. (60 ml or ¼ cup) strong cocoa drink

2 oz. (60 ml or ¼ cup) chocolate infused vegetable oils. To make your own add ½ cup cacao nibs to 1 cup of a vegetable oil like sweet almond oil, olive or sunflower oil. Leave the mixture in a bright sunny place for two to six weeks as you shake it daily – the longer you leave it the stronger it gets. Strain the mixture with a cheese cloth and use the oil in your recipe.

1 teaspoon vitamin E oil (optional natural preservative)

Follow the above Basic Face Wash Recipe Instructions.

* * * * *

5

VEGETABLE OILS

Choose the vegetable oils you will use for your face cleanser depending on the characteristics of the oil.

Sweet Almond Oil

Sweet almond oil contains vitamins A, B, E, minerals and skin nourishing essential fatty acids. It is especially beneficial for normal skin, dry skin, sensitive skin, mature skin and eczema prone skin.

Do not use sweet almond oil if you have nut allergy.

***

Sunflower Oil

Sunflower oil contains vitamin A, E and skin nourishing essential fatty acids. It is especially beneficial for normal skin and dry skin.

***

Avocado Oil

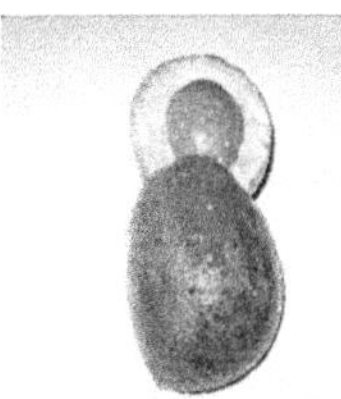

Avocado oil is rich in skin nourishing nutrients. It is especially beneficial for normal skin, dry skin, sensitive skin, mature skin, eczema prone skin and psoriasis prone skin.

***

Apricot Kernel Oil

Apricot kernel oil contains vitamins A, E, minerals and skin nourishing essential fatty acids. It is especially beneficial for dry skin, sensitive skin, mature skin and prematurely aging skin.

***

Jojoba

Jojoba is a plant wax which contains vitamin E, proteins, minerals, fatty acids and protective antioxidants. It is beneficial for normal, mature, oily or acne prone skin, eczema and psoriasis prone skin.

***

Olive Oil

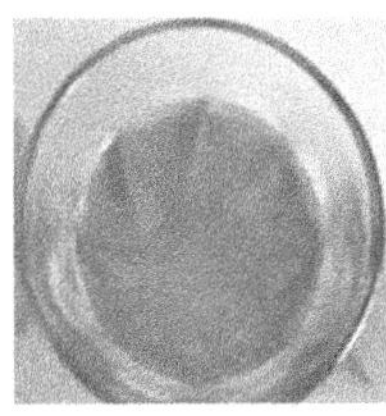

Olive oil contains skin nourishing essential fatty acids and natural sunscreens. It is especially beneficial for dry skin, mature skin and eczema prone skin. It is also conditions nails.

Virgin Coconut Oil

Virgin coconut oil contains skin nourishing fatty acids. It is especially beneficial for dry skin. It also conditions nails.

***

Fractionated Coconut Oil

Fractionated coconut oil is especially beneficial for dry skin and sensitive skin.

***

Canola Oil

Canola oil is especially beneficial for normal skin, dry skin, sensitive skin and mature skin.

***

Evening Primrose Oil

Evening primrose oil contains skin nourishing essential fatty acids, vitamins and minerals. It is especially beneficial for dry skin, mature skin, eczema prone skin and psoriasis prone skin.

* * * * *

6

ESSENTIAL OILS

Choose the essential oils you will use for your natural products depending on the properties of that aromatherapy oil.

Clary Sage Essential Oil

Clary Sage Essential Oil has an herbaceous scent. It can help relieve stress related tension, reduce irritability and help one relax. It is also used for the management of mature and acne prone skin.

Do not use it during pregnancy or if you are drinking alcohol or driving or if you have endometriosis, ovarian cysts, uterine cysts, breast cancer or you are at high risk for developing breast cancer as it may have an "estrogen-like" effect on the body.

***

Eucalyptus Essential Oil

Eucalyptus essential oil has an invigorating scent. It can help relieve stress related mental tension and mental exhaustion. It is also used in the management of joint aches and pains.

Do not use eucalyptus essential oil if you have epilepsy, high blood pressure or apply it near a baby's nostrils.

***

Geranium Essential Oil

Geranium Essential Oil has a fresh, minty rose scent. It can help relieve nervous tension and anxiety. It is also used in the management of eczema, cellulite as well as mature skin. Avoid using it in pregnancy.

***

Grapefruit Essential Oil

Grapefruit essential oil has a refreshing, bitter-sweet scent. It can help relieve tension and release repressed emotions. It is also used in the management of cellulite.

***

Lavender Essential Oil

Lavender essential oil has a soothing, floral scent. It can help one relax and relieve stress related tension, sleeplessness, anxiety and depression. It is also used in the management of acne, eczema and dry skin conditions.

Do not use lavender essential oil in pregnancy, if you are breastfeeding, on young children as it may cause breast development in young boys and girls. Avoid it if you have low blood pressure as you may feel drowsy after using it.

***

Lemon Essential Oil

Lemon essential oil has a clarifying fresh scent. It can help relieve mental tension, alleviate mental fatigue and increase concentration. It is also used in the management of acne and post acne dark skin spots.

Do not use it if skin will be exposed to sunlight or UV rays in the next 12-24 hours. Do not use it if you have low blood pressure or you are allergic to lemons.

***

Lemongrass Essential Oil

Lemongrass essential oil has a vitalizing, lemony scent. It helps relieve tension and muscle aches. It is also used in the management of acne.

Do not use it if skin will be exposed to sunlight or UV rays in the next 12-24 hours.

***

Roman Chamomile Essential Oil

Roman chamomile essential oil has a sweet and fruity scent. It can help relieve stress related tension headaches. It is also used in the management of eczema, psoriasis and dry skin conditions.

Avoid using it in pregnancy and if you are allergic to ragweed.

***

Spearmint Essential Oil

Spearmint essential oil has a gently-energizing minty scent. It can help relieve mental tension and exhaustion. It is also used to manage nausea.

***

Rose Essential Oil

Rose essential oil has a sweet and floral scent. It has mentally cheering properties and is used to relieve depression, sorrow and heartache. It is also useful for mature and prematurely aging skin.

***

Rosemary Essential Oil

Rosemary Essential Oil has an uplifting and stimulating scent. It can help relieve mental exhaustion and feeling rundown. It is also used in the management of dry skin, eczema, muscle aches and joint pains.

Do not use rosemary essential oil if you are pregnant or have epilepsy or high blood pressure. Avoid using it if you have a fever or you want to sleep and in children under 5 years.

***

Sweet Orange Essential Oil

Sweet orange essential oil has a cheeringly, refreshing scent. It can help mange stress related tension. It is also used in the management of cellulite and common colds.

Do not use it if skin will be exposed to sunlight or UV rays in the next 12-24 hours.

***

Peppermint Essential Oil

Peppermint essential oil has a head-clearing, refreshing scent. It can help relieve tension and fatigue. It is also used to manage flatulence.

Do not use peppermint essential oil in pregnancy, if breastfeeding, on children less than 5 years, if you have epilepsy or irregular heartbeats or cardiac fibrillation or high blood pressure and before using a sun bed or going to hot humid places.

***

Tea Tree Essential Oil

Tea tree essential oil has a purifying almost medicinal scent. It can help relieve tension and fatigue. It is also been used in the management of oily skin, acne and athlete's foot.

***

Ylang Ylang Essential Oil

Ylang ylang essential oil has a fragrantly floral scent. It can help relieve anxiety, tension and help one relax. It is also used as an aphrodisiac and in the management of dry skin conditions.

Do not use ylang ylang essential oil if you have low blood pressure or sensitive, damaged skin.

*****

7

SKIN FOOD

Choose the food items you will use for your natural products depending on your skin type and the condition you want to manage.

Aloe Vera Gel

Aloe vera has anti-inflammatory properties and it soothes inflamed skin. It also stimulates cell regeneration and is vital for healing. Aloe is also an excellent moisturizer since it contains over 90% water,

Apples

Apples are great for the skin because they contain 85% water and vitamins A and C. These vitamins are potent antioxidants which protect the skin cells from the free radical damage that contributes to premature aging. Apples also contain malic acid which is great for exfoliating and removing dead cells from the skin's surface.

***

Coffee

Coffee is an excellent exfoliant which removes the dead cells on the surface of the skin. It also contains the anti-inflammatory caffeic acid which is also said to increase skin's collagen production.

***

Honey

Honey has antiseptic activity which is useful for controlling infections and healing the skin. It is also a humectant which helps keep the skin moisturized. Honey also softens the skin. In addition, it is also a powerful antioxidant which is useful for preventing free radical damage to skin cells that causes premature aging.

***

Lemon

Lemon contains natural acids which aid in exfoliation and lightening dark marks like acne scars. It can also be used as a toner for oily skin.

***

Milk

Milk regardless of whether it is whole, skimmed or buttermilk, contains lactic acid, which is an alpha hydroxy acid (AHA), that helps slough away the dead cells on the surface of the skin. In addition, milk products help the skin retain its moisture as they gently exfoliate it.

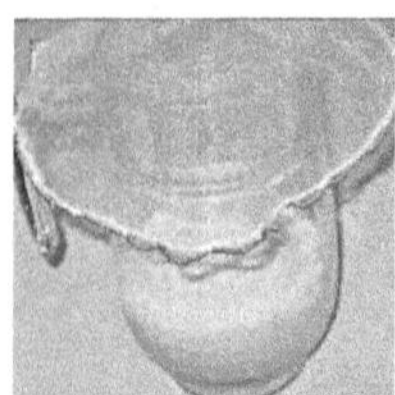

***

Neem

Neem is an effective skin antiseptic which kills bacteria and soothes inflammation without further irritating the skin.

*****

8

NATURAL PRESERVATIVES

Natural preservatives used to make skin care products include:

Rosemary Oleoresin

Rosemary oleoresin, which is also known as ROE, is a natural antioxidant extracted from the rosemary herb. It contains carnosic acid which extends the shelf life of homemade products by reducing the oxidation of their natural ingredients.

***

Vitamin E Oil

Vitamin E oil which usually comes as a mixture of tocopherols is natural antioxidant extracted from vegetable oils. Vitamin E oil is heat stable and can be used to extend the shelf life of products which do not contain water.

Grapefruit Seed Extract

Grapefruit seed extract is rich in vitamins C and E which are natural antioxidants. It is also able to kill or inhibit the growth of bacteria and fungi. It therefore functions both as a broad spectrum preservative and as an antioxidant.

###

ABOUT THE AUTHOR

Dr. Miriam Kinai is a medical doctor and a certified clinical aromatherapy practitioner.

You can visit her blog at http://www.MyBlogBookClub.com or follow her on twitter at http://twitter.com/AlmasiHealth

Email enquiries to almasihealthcare@yahoo.com with BOOKS as your subject.

HOW TO MAKE NATURAL SKIN CARE PRODUCTS SERIES

Books in this series include:

* How to Make Natural Bath and Body Oils

* How to Make Natural Bath Bombs

* How to Make Natural Bath Cookies

* How to Make Natural Bath Melts

* How to Make Natural Bath Milks

* How to Make Natural Bath Salts

* How to Make Natural Bath Teas

* How to make Natural Loofa Soap

* How to Make Natural Body Butters

* How to Make Natural Body Lotions

* How to Make Natural Body Scrubs

* How to Make Natural Body Wash

* How to Make Natural Healing Balms

* How to Make Natural Face Cleansers

* How to Make Natural Face Masks

* How to Make Natural Face Scrubs

* How to Make Natural Cold Cream

* How to Make Natural Anti-Wrinkle Creams and Anti-Aging Serums

* How to Make Natural Foot Scrubs

* How to Make Natural Foot Deodorizers

* How to Make Natural Foot Balms

* How to Make Natural Pumice Foot Soap

* How to Make Natural Shampoos

* How to Make Natural Hair Conditioners

* How to Make Natural Hair Gel

* How to Make Natural Hair Rinse

* How to Make Natural Hot Oil Hair Treatment

* How to Make Natural Hair Dye

* How to Make Natural Hair Balm

* How to Make Natural Hair Removal Gel

* How to Make Natural Anti-Cellulite Soap

* How to Make Natural Anti-Cellulite Cream

* How to Make Natural Anti-Cellulite Lotion

* How to Make Natural Anti-Cellulite Wraps

*****

* How to Make Natural Soap

* How to Make Natural Solid and Liquid Castile Soap

* How to make Natural Cosmetics

* How to Make Natural Solid and Liquid Perfumes

* How to Make Natural Toothpaste, Tooth Whitening Powder and Mouthwash

* How to Make Natural Sunscreen Lotions

* How to make Natural Insect Repellent

* How to Make Natural Herb Infused Oils

* How to Make Natural Massage Bars

* How to Make Ubtan Powder

*****

THE QUICK GOURMET CHEF

The Quick Gourmet is an essential culinary skills cookbook which teaches how to make simple, divine dishes.

You will learn how to make:

* Hot Chocolate Mixes and Drinks

* Hot Chai Tea Mixes and Drinks

* Hot Coffee Mixes and Drinks

* Sensational Smoothies

* Non-Dairy Smoothies

* Chocolate Covered Strawberries

* Chocolate Truffles

* Healthy Chicken Salads

* Healthy Tuna Salads

* Savory Salsas

* Herb Butter

* Cheese Dips and Sauces

* Gourmet Sandwiches

* Perfect Hard Boiled Eggs

* A Cheese Board

* Natural Food Color

*****

AROMATHERAPY COURSE

Aromatherapy Course by Dr Miriam Kinai tutors you on how to use essential oils to improve your physical, mental and emotional well being.

The author's experience as a medical doctor and clinical aromatherapy practitioner have enabled her to create a highly informative course on how to use these natural plant essences.

You will learn:

* The safety information and therapeutic uses of essential oils like clary sage, eucalyptus, geranium, grapefruit, lavender, lemon, lemongrass, marjoram, orange (sweet), patchouli, peppermint, Roman chamomile, rose, rosemary, sandalwood, spearmint, tea tree and ylang ylang.

* The safety information and therapeutic uses of carrier oils like apricot kernel oil, avocado oil, borage seed oil, calendula oil, carrot seed oil, castor oil, evening primrose oil, fractionated coconut oil, jojoba, olive oil, rosehip oil, sunflower oil, sweet almond oil and virgin coconut oil.

* How to blend essential oils

* How to dilute essential oils with carrier oils

* How to administer essential oils

* How to make natural healing products from numerous aromatherapy recipes

* How to utilize the healing benefits of essentials oils even if you do not have prior training in aromatherapy

The Aromatherapy Course will leave you with a clear understanding of how you can heal yourself and your family naturally by using essentials oils on your body and in your home.

*****

CHRISTIAN LIFE COACHING HANDBOOK

Christian Life Coaching Handbook offers a Biblical approach to managing different aspects of life.

You will learn:

* Christian anger management

* Christian conflict resolution

* Christian depression treatment

* Christian goal setting

* Christian marital stress management

* Christian stress management

* How to assert yourself

* How to defeat fear

* How to love yourself

* How to overcome shyness

* How to resist temptation

* How to stop being a people pleaser

*****

CHRISTIAN SPIRITUAL WARFARE

Christian Spiritual Warfare teaches you the awesome Bible verses you can use as spiritual warfare prayers, Christian affirmations and in your Christian meditation sessions as you fight your spiritual battles.

You will learn how to fight for the following with Bible verses:

* Marriage * Children * Health

* Christian Faith * Christian Ministry

* Country

* Finances * Job * Business

* Peace of Mind * Restoration * Self Esteem * Self Love

You will also learn how to fight against the following with Bible verses:

* Addiction * Temptation

* Being Single * Infertility

* Opposition * Oppression

* Worry * Fear

* Feelings of Condemnation * Confusion

* Danger * Death * Despair * Discouragement

* Impatience * Insomnia * Laziness * Loneliness

* Poverty * Pride * Sadness

* Vengeance * Weakness

* A Foul Mouth * Lying

*****

DARK SKIN DERMATOLOGY COLOR ATLAS

Dark Skin Dermatology Color Atlas is filled with clear explanations and color photos of skin, hair, and nail diseases affecting people with skin of color or Fitzpatrick skin types IV, V, and VI.

Topics covered include Acne Vulgaris, Alopecia Areata, Anal Warts, Angioedema, Aphthous Ulcers, Atopic Dermatitis, Blastomycosis, Blister Beetle Dermatitis or Nairobi Fly Dermatitis, Cellulitis, Chronic Ulcers, Confetti Hypopigmentation, Cutaneous T Cell Lymphoma, Cutaneous Tuberculosis, Dermatitis Artefacta, Erythema Nodosum,

Exfoliative Erythroderma, Gianotti Crosti Syndrome, Hand Dermatitis, Hemangioma, Herpes Zoster, Ichthyosis, Ingrown Toenails, Irritant Contact Dermatitis, Kaposi Sarcoma, Keloids, Keratoderma Blenorrhagica, Klippel Trenaunay Weber Syndrome, Leishmaniasis, Leprosy, Leukonychia, Lichen Nitidus, Lichen Planus,

Lichenoid Drug Eruption, Linear Epidermal Nevus, Linear IgA Dermatosis (LAD), Lipodermatosclerosis, Lymphangioma Circumscriptum, Miliaria, Molluscum Contagiosum, Neurofibromatosis, Nickel Dermatitis, Onychomadesis, Onychomycosis, Palmoplantar Eccrine Hidradenitis, Papular Pruritic Eruption (PPE), Paronychia, Pellagra, Pemphigus Foliaceous,

Pemphigus Vulgaris, Piebaldism, Pityriasis Rosea, Pityriasis Rubra Pilaris, Plantar Hyperkeratosis, Plantar Warts, Poikiloderma, Postinflammatory Hyperpigmentation and Hypopigmentation, Post Topical Steroids Hypopigmentation, Psoriasis, Pyogenic Granuloma or Lobular Capillary Hemangioma, Scabies, Seborrheic Dermatitis, Steven Johnson Syndrome (SJS) and Toxic Epidermal Necrolysis (TEN),

Sunburn, Systemic Sclerosis, Tinea Capitis, Tinea Pedis, Tinea Versicolor, Traction Alopecia, Urticaria, Vasculitis, Vitiligo, and Xanthelasma.

*****